P

by Kris Bonnell

Pumpkin seeds grow into a pumpkin vine.

3

Flowers grow on the vine.

Little green pumpkins grow under the flowers.

The little green pumpkins grow into big green pumpkins.

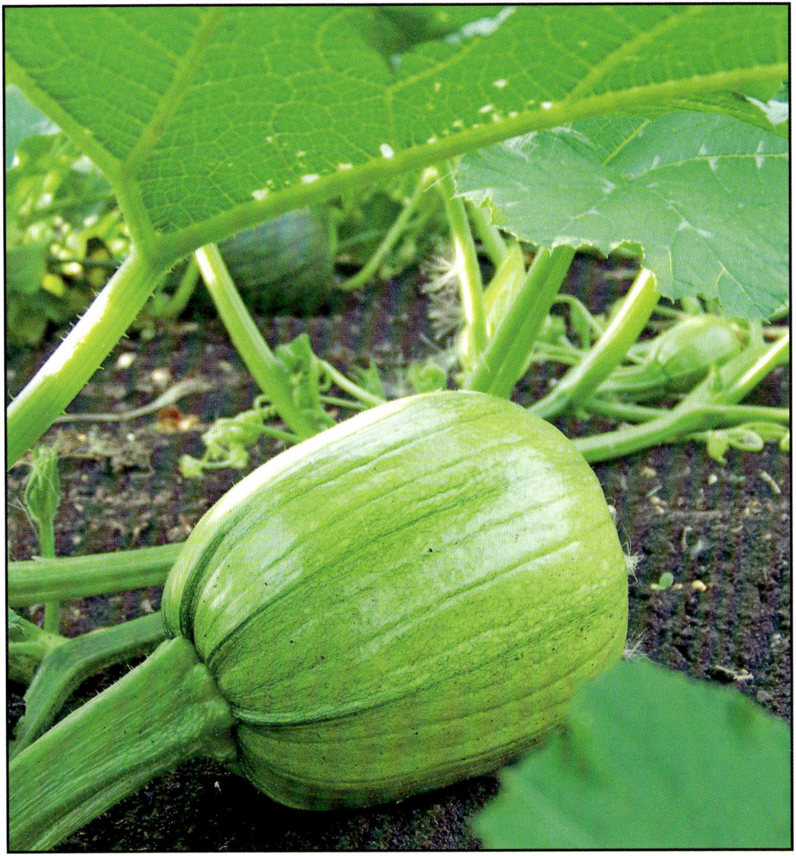

The green pumpkins become orange pumpkins.

9

Look at the top
of this pumpkin.

The old vine becomes the stem.

Look at the end
of the pumpkin.

This is the old flower.

# The old flower falls off.

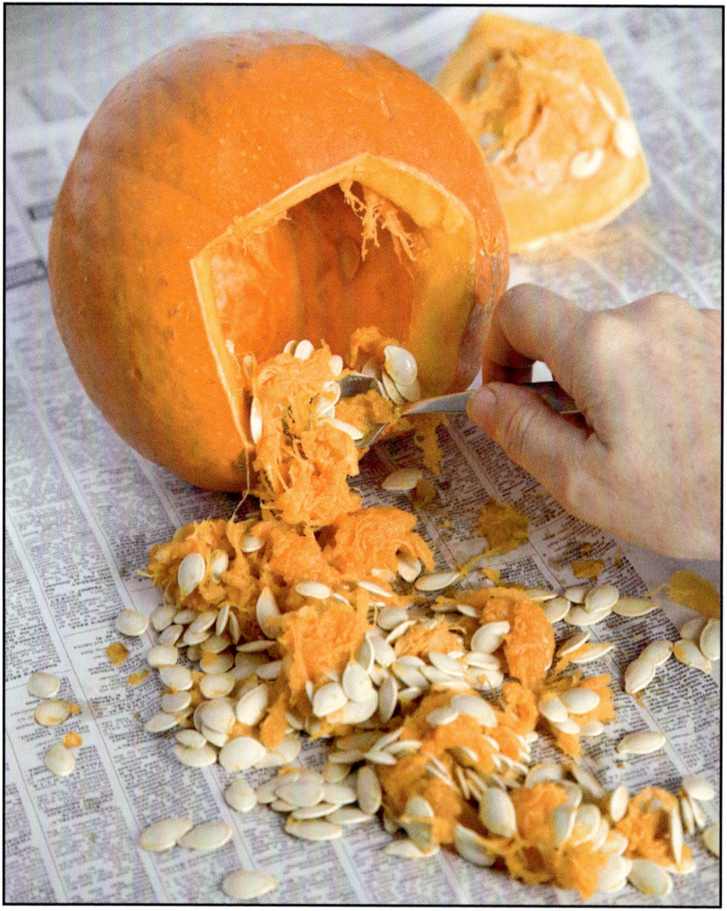

Pumpkin seeds are inside a pumpkin.

The seeds will become new pumpkins.

seeds

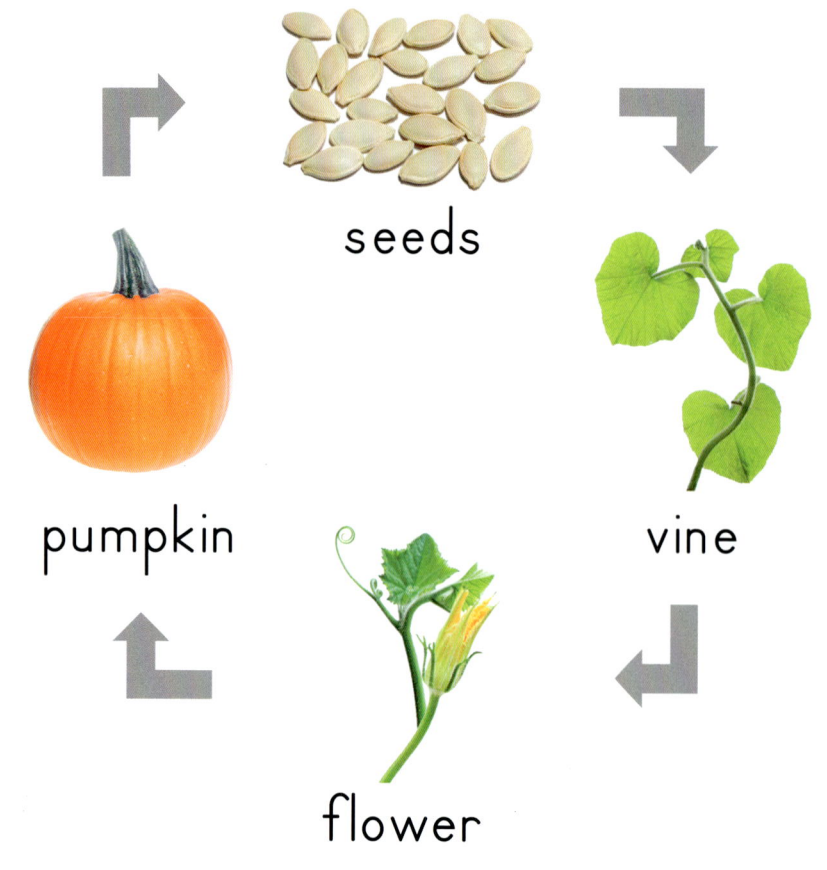

vine

flower

pumpkin